SAFE & SOUND

Our Health

Wendy Conklin, M.A.

Consultants

Timothy Rasinski, Ph.D.
Kent State University

Lori Oczkus, M.A.
Literacy Consultant

Kimberly Kilpatrick, M.S., R.D.
Registered Dietitian

Publishing Credits

Rachelle Cracchiolo, M.S.Ed., *Publisher*
Conni Medina, M.A.Ed., *Managing Editor*
Dona Herweck Rice, *Series Developer*
Emily R. Smith, M.A.Ed., *Content Director*
Stephanie Bernard/Noelle Cristea, M.A.Ed., *Editors*
Robin Erickson, *Senior Graphic Designer*

The TIME logo is a registered trademark of TIME Inc. Used under license.

Image Credits: p.13 (left) Valuavitaly/Dreamstime.com, (right) Alexmax/Dreamstime.com; pp.14–15 Jim West/ Alamy Stock Photo; pp.18–19 age fotostock/Alamy Stock Photo; pp.26–27 Jordan Siemens/Getty Images; p.30 LOC [LC-DIG-ppmsca-15835]; p.31 (top) LOC [LC-DIG-ppmsca-15886], (bottom right) LOC [LC-DIG-cwpb-04407], (bottom left) LOC [LC-USZ62-104949]; all other images from iStock and/or Shutterstock

Library of Congress Cataloging-in-Publication Data

Names: Conklin, Wendy, author.
Title: Safe & sound : our health / Wendy Conklin, M.A.
Other titles: Safe and sound : Our Health | Our Health
Description: Huntington Beach, CA : Teacher Created Materials, [2017] | Audience: Grades 7 to 8. | Includes index.
Identifiers: LCCN 2016048468 (print) | LCCN 2016049770 (ebook) | ISBN 9781493836291 (pbk.) | ISBN 9781480757332 (eBook)
Subjects: LCSH: Health behavior in adolescence--Juvenile literature. | Nutrition--Juvenile literature. | Exercise--Juvenile literature. | Health--Juvenile literature.
Classification: LCC RJ47.53 .C67 2017 (print) | LCC RJ47.53 (ebook) | DDC 613/.0433--dc23
LC record available at https://lccn.loc.gov/2016048468

Teacher Created Materials

5301 Oceanus Drive
Huntington Beach, CA 92649-1030
http://www.tcmpub.com

ISBN 978-1-4938-3629-1

Table of Contents

Forming Your Identity

In the book *Alice's Adventures in Wonderland*, Alice asks, "Who in the world am I? Ah, *that's* the great puzzle." Right now, you are developing your identity. Your identity is determined by what you think about yourself, how you treat other people, what you believe is important, and many, many other things.

Defining *You*

Your identity is shaped by what you do and why you do it. Think about what you stand for, how you choose friends, and how you want others to perceive you. Knowing the answers to these questions can be hard, but once you've defined all the parts that make you *you*, it is easier to lead a life that reflects your values.

You are valuable no matter what others may say or what your mind may try to convince you of at times—and you are unique. The things you do today, such as what you eat, how you think, and the people you form relationships with, can have big impacts on your future. Sometimes it is difficult to think too far into the future because so much is going on in your life. Homework, chores, family, and fun activities might seem like a lot of priorities to juggle.

The most important thing you can do as you develop your identity is to take care of yourself so that you—your mind and your body—are healthy.

Having a strong sense of self is the most important thing to focus on at this point in your life. How you think, how you feel, and how you interact with others make up the real you, and these things help you determine your personal values.

To develop your true sense of self, search for things you are passionate about and then throw yourself into them. If you are passionate about basketball, acting, or painting, spend time doing those things, and give them all you've got. Try different activities and hobbies until you find something that fits, or get involved in various causes. Donate your time to helping others who are in need. This could be in the form of tutoring a struggling student, volunteering at a local pet shelter, or cleaning the yard of an elderly neighbor. Volunteering and finding your passion will help form your true sense of self over time.

Trying New Things

You might already have a hobby or activity that you love. But it's important to branch out and try new things—even those you think you might not enjoy. Trying new hobbies and activities helps you figure out who you are. Who knows? You might end up liking something you never thought you would.

How Food Affects Your Body

Your diet affects you in many different ways, including your weight, height, concentration, and skin complexion. Dietary advice typically includes *what* you should eat and *how much* you should eat to be healthy.

The most important thing to remember about food is to eat a balanced, healthy diet. This means making sure you get enough protein (such as lean beef, chicken, fish, or tofu), carbohydrates (such as fruits, vegetables, or whole grains), and healthy fats (found in foods such as nuts or avocado) with every meal. Protein builds muscle and is part of every cell in your body. Fat stores energy and protects your nerve cells. Carbohydrates give your body energy throughout the day. Eating a balance of these three **macronutrients** will help you maintain a healthy weight and keep your body energized and working well.

Also, don't forget about drinking water to stay hydrated. Try to avoid sugary foods and drinks as much as possible because they won't provide your body with the nutrients it needs.

Diet Details

The word *diet* is often used to describe consuming or avoiding certain foods in an effort to lose weight. But the word *diet* also describes the foods and drinks you consume on a regular basis, even if you have no plan to lose weight. So don't automatically assume that *diet* means someone wants to lose weight.

THINK LINK

- Think about how you normally eat. What about your diet would change if you followed these suggestions about eating a balanced, healthy diet?

- Why do you think some people shy away from eating fats if they are trying to lose weight?

- Why is it important to get all the macronutrients in a meal?

Sugar Rush

Foods high in **refined** sugar can cause people to gain weight because sugar is a type of carbohydrate (or carb), and eating too many carbs without enough activity can cause weight gain and increase susceptibility to diseases. Your body breaks down carbs in different ways. There are two kinds—**simple carbohydrates** (sometimes called simple sugars), which can be found in ice cream, sodas, and fruit, and **complex carbohydrates**, which can be found in starchy vegetables and whole-grain bread.

Simple carbs rush into your bloodstream as soon as they are consumed, and because they are digested quickly, you feel the effects immediately. You get a rush of energy and feel good quickly. But because your body digests the simple carbs so fast, that feeling does not last long. Once the sugar is broken down, your body craves that rush again. This often leads to eating more simple carbs, creating a cycle.

On the other hand, complex carbs take longer to break down, and they contain vitamins and nutrients your body needs. Complex carbs slowly release into your blood stream, so you don't feel the highs and lows of having too much or too little energy.

Natural vs. Processed

Simple sugars can be found in natural sources such as fruits and dairy products. These types of simple sugars are better for you than refined or processed sugars because they contain essential nutrients. Processed sugars, such as the ones found in candy, cakes, syrups, and sodas, should be consumed only in moderation.

Apples or Apple Juice?

Have you ever noticed that apple juice has more **calories** than an apple? This is because juice is a concentrated source of fruit sugar. It doesn't have pulp or skin to add fiber and slow the digestion of the sugar. So, if given the choice, pick the apple—your body will thank you.

How Much Should I Eat?

You might be wondering *how much* you should eat to be healthy. Most teens need at least 2,000 calories per day since their bodies are growing at such rapid rates. These calories should be spread out over multiple meals. No matter if you prefer to eat three large meals a day or six small ones, the important thing is to make sure you are getting enough calories from healthy food sources in each meal.

One of the easiest tricks to figuring out how much to eat is to use your hands as measuring devices. The palm of your hand is roughly how much protein you should eat at a meal. The size of your fist equals one serving of fruit or vegetables. The fist is also an excellent tool for helping you measure a serving of brown rice or whole-grain pasta. A handful of nuts is equivalent to about one ounce and will provide you with a good amount of healthy fat. Or you can try a teaspoon of olive oil (tip of your thumb) or a tablespoon of avocado (your whole thumb) with every meal to get the healthy fat you need.

While monitoring portion size is a knowledgeable way to ensure you're not eating too much, it's more important to simply focus on making healthy choices by eating from each of the five food groups.

Fat Is *Good* for You?!

The average teen brain needs about 25 percent of its daily calories from fat to give it the maximum capacity for learning. Without good fats from sources such as avocado, nuts, and olive oil, your brain capacity actually shrinks, which interferes with your ability to think and learn. So, be sure to steer clear of trans fat, and spread the good fats throughout the day.

The Dangers of Not Eating

You might think that not eating is a quick way to lose some extra weight. However, when you don't eat, you are starving your body of the essential nutrients it needs to function properly. If you are overweight, the healthiest way to lose weight is eating a balanced diet, limiting sugar intake, and getting daily exercise.

fist = 1 cup

thumb tip = 1 tsp.

palm = 3 oz.

thumb = 1 tbs.

STOP! THINK....

- ⊚ Why might it be helpful to use your hands as measuring tools?
- ⊚ How would you explain the recommended portion size to someone who thinks all fat is bad?

Exercise Is Good for You

Many people promote the physical benefits of exercise. While it's certainly true that exercise can make you better at sports and keep your body healthy, it has other benefits as well. Whether you run track, play volleyball, or march in the band, exercise is good for both your body *and* your mind.

How Exercise Helps Your Mind

Have you ever noticed that after you exercise, you may be physically tired, but you actually feel better overall or have more energy? This happens because exercise releases **endorphins**. As a result, you experience a more positive attitude and good mood. In the same way, exercise also helps relieve stress because endorphins aid in easing those stressful feelings. So, if you are feeling down or stressed out, one of the best ways to improve your mood is to exercise.

Strong Muscles, Strong Bones

Lifting weights not only increases muscle size but also helps you build stronger bones. You can help maximize your bone density by exercising and getting enough vitamin D and calcium.

How Exercise Helps Your Body

When a doctor says that someone is overweight, it means that the person has excess fat on his or her body. Obesity is a condition of excess body fat and can come with many health problems, including joint pain, diabetes, heart disease, and high blood pressure.

Exercise helps your body in several ways. Moving your body keeps your **metabolism** active. Having an active metabolism means that your body burns more calories throughout the day. Exercise also builds up your muscles so that they become fat-burning machines to help you burn calories. So after exercising, your body continues to burn calories— even when you are sitting around.

You've probably noticed how your heart beats faster when you run or partake in **vigorous** exercise. This happens because movement burns **glucose**. More oxygen is required to burn glucose, so your heart has to pump more oxygen-rich blood to your muscle tissue. And the more you challenge your heart through exercise, the stronger it will become.

Lean Mass

You may have heard that muscle weighs more than fat— but actually muscle is denser than fat. A pound of fat weighs the same as a pound of muscle; but muscle takes up less space than fat does. So, you might work out and lose fat but weigh the same as before, or even more. Do not let the scale rule your life—an increase in weight might mean you are gaining lean body mass and losing fat.

Staying Safe as You Exercise

Perhaps you already exercise regularly by participating in sports, such as basketball, softball, soccer, or football. If this is true for you, it's important to understand that it is possible to push your body *too* far during physical activity. Certain sports can be very demanding on the body and can put joints, muscles, and other body parts at risk of injury. For example, baseball pitchers can overuse their shoulder joints and risk tearing their **rotator cuffs**. A tennis or football player can tear the **meniscus** by quickly changing direction on the court or field.

To avoid injury, it's important to make sure you don't overuse these parts of your body. Also, be sure to warm up before you practice or play. This will keep your muscles from pulling and straining. Wear the appropriate gear for the sport, such as cleats, a helmet, or protective padding. Finally, eat plenty of protein and drink lots of water. Your body needs both of these things to recover after a workout.

The Truth about Sports Drinks

Sports drinks contain carbohydrates and **electrolytes** that help replenish what your body loses in sweat during a tough workout. But these should only be consumed if you have lost *a lot* of sweat. Truthfully, sports drinks are not needed because all the nutrients and hydration you need can be fulfilled with healthy eating and drinking habits. You won't need to worry about consuming sports drinks if you drink plenty of water before, during, and after exercise.

Prepare Your Muscles

A good warm-up should include **dynamic stretches** and movements such as jumping jacks, push-ups, sit-ups, and jogging. To prevent soreness, you should only do **static stretches** after exercise, while your body is still warm.

rotator cuff

meniscus

The Power of Stress

You might hear your friends describe themselves as "stressed out," and you may sometimes feel that way, too. Stress is an unavoidable part of life, and it can come in many different forms. But have you ever thought of stress as a good thing? Think about it—everyone lives with low-level stress. You might have responsibilities like mowing the lawn, finishing homework, or walking the dog. These small stressors of everyday life help you develop a sense of responsibility.

Stress can also set in because of deadlines—the nagging things that we have to complete by certain times. Deadlines help people get things done while also forcing people to solve problems and think creatively in a given amount of time. If we had all the time in the world, we might not get anything done, so sometimes stress is a good motivator. Remember that while some stress is normal, even helpful, it's important to ask for support if you are feeling overwhelmed.

Then there's the stress that arises from a major life change. During these big life changes, such as changing schools or recovering from a serious illness, it's especially important to take care of yourself. You might also talk through your feelings with a trustworthy friend or adult.

Time Management Tip

Try managing the responsibilities of homework with a schedule broken into blocks of time. For example, block one hour for math homework or studying. Turn off your phone, and find a quiet place so you can focus for that hour. Then, schedule 15–30 minutes for a break—get something to eat, talk to friends, or watch television. Repeat these steps until all your work is complete.

Study Tips

Research shows that by teaching others a concept, you learn it better yourself. Also, putting information into a song or poem makes the information easier to remember. Prepare and take sample tests before the big one in class. Finally, connect the information to something in real life so that you can remember it more easily.

Have you ever experienced an emergency that caused your heart to race and made you feel like you had superhuman strength? That was your adrenal gland producing a **hormone** called **adrenaline**. When you are under stress, your brain produces a variety of chemicals, including adrenaline, that go through the bloodstream to other parts of your body. Simultaneously, the adrenal glands also produce a hormone called **cortisol**. This gives your muscles and brain the energy to react as needed to the situation. When the stress ends, the cortisol travels back to the brain and tells it to stop producing the stress hormones. Then, your body is supposed to go back to normal.

For some people, however, this stress does not end. As a result, they experience health problems, such as panic attacks or trouble sleeping. It's important to learn to manage stress so that you don't experience the negative effects of it. Be sure to eat healthy foods, get enough sleep, exercise, and find healthy ways to relax, such as breathing techniques or meditation. If you still have trouble, be sure to talk to your doctor about your stress levels.

Stress Relief

Managing stress takes effort and practice with listening to your body. When you feel stressed, decompress by going for a walk or run. Take part in a hobby you enjoy, such as reading or creating something. Some people relieve stress alone, and some let off steam better with friends. Choose the option that works best for you!

THINK LINK

- When people don't manage their stress, they experience health problems. How do these problems affect a person's life on a daily basis?

- How do the body and the brain work together to manage a stressful situation?

Your Healthy Brain

Your brain controls everything—how you feel, how you act, and what you say—so it's imperative that you take good care of it. At times, you might feel a little blue or depressed. Don't worry; this is a normal feeling every now and then. You won't always feel as though you are on top of the world. Sometimes things go wrong, and it's completely normal for that to affect how you feel or your overall outlook. But it's important to distinguish between these typical feelings of sadness and more serious situations where assistance may be needed to feel better.

Here's what happens in your brain that affects how you feel. The amygdala (uh-MIG-duh-luh) is a section of your brain containing your emotions, and it communicates to the **prefrontal cortex**. So, if you were to see lightning strike close by, your amygdala would send the message to your prefrontal cortex that it is scary and dangerous. Then, your prefrontal cortex tells you to take cover inside a safe building. Your amygdala is constantly sending messages to your cortex, and this is why you feel frightened, depressed, happy, or excited at different times.

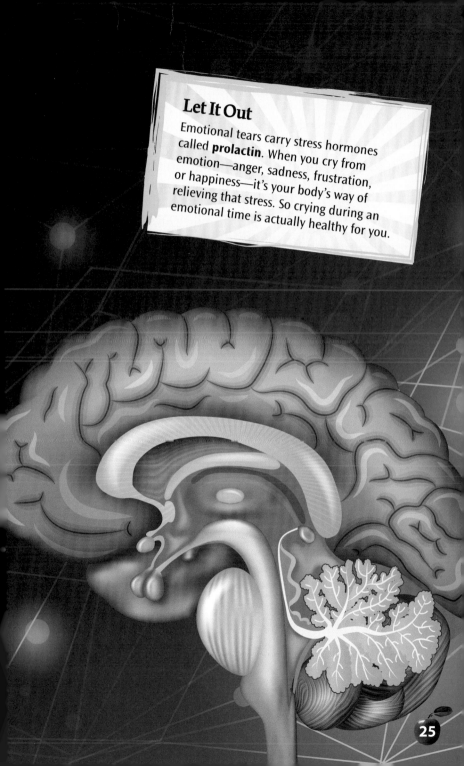

Let It Out

Emotional tears carry stress hormones called **prolactin**. When you cry from emotion—anger, sadness, frustration, or happiness—it's your body's way of relieving that stress. So crying during an emotional time is actually healthy for you.

Finding Balance

You might feel on top of the world when you win an art competition. And, on the contrary, you might feel really sad when you end a relationship with someone. These are normal emotions that everyone experiences at one time or another, and they are the result of your brain reacting to the situation at hand. However, there are some things you can do to help limit the negative effects these emotions have on your mind.

You can release good chemicals into your body through exercise. Even as little as five minutes of exercise has been shown to improve people's moods. And while you are at it, select a beautiful place, such as a beach or a park, in which to exercise. Research shows that beautiful places combined with exertion calm the mind and help relieve stress.

Another thing you can do to help counteract negative emotions is to eat healthy. Most of the time, our immediate reaction when feeling down is to reach for salty chips, sugary cookies, or fried foods, but these foods only give a sugar rush that helps momentarily and leaves you feeling worse afterward. Doctors have found that there are "good mood foods" that help us to feel better for a much longer time because they maintain blood-sugar levels and feed the brain the right nutrients.

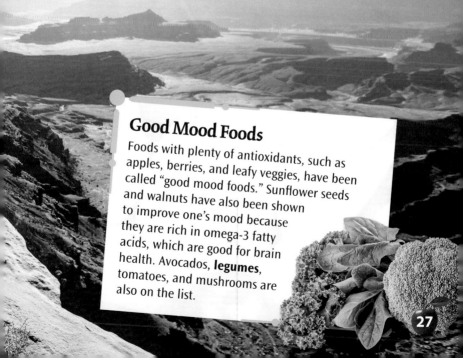

Good Mood Foods

Foods with plenty of antioxidants, such as apples, berries, and leafy veggies, have been called "good mood foods." Sunflower seeds and walnuts have also been shown to improve one's mood because they are rich in omega-3 fatty acids, which are good for brain health. Avocados, **legumes**, tomatoes, and mushrooms are also on the list.

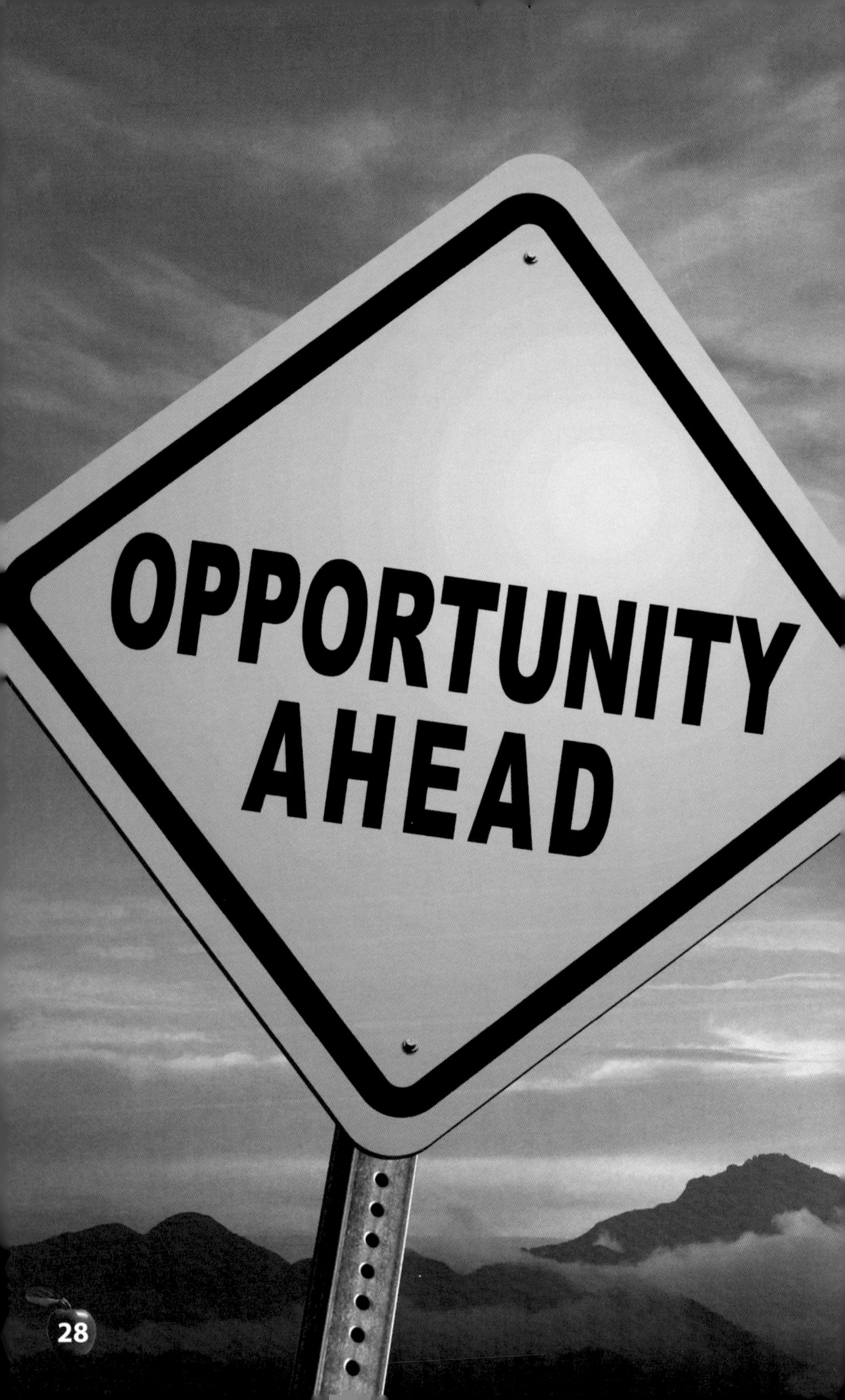
OPPORTUNITY
AHEAD

Think Positive Thoughts

Your thoughts affect your life. Many studies show that by thinking positive thoughts, the brain becomes better at fighting disease and managing stress.

In the same way, your thoughts can also sabotage your potential success. Comparing yourself to others or thinking negative thoughts about yourself doesn't bring positivity to your life, nor does it help manage stress or unfavorable situations. If you say to yourself, "I'm the *worst* batter in the world. I never hit the ball hard enough to get on base," you may start to believe it and feel as though you will never improve. On the other hand, you don't need to lie to yourself, either, by saying, "I'm the *greatest* home-run hitter in the world!" Instead, remind yourself that while you may not be the best batter, the more you practice, the better you will become.

Daily Affirmations

One form of positive thinking is a daily affirmation. Many people use daily affirmations across the world. An affirmation is a way to assert something positive, either to yourself or someone else. Here are some common ones you may have heard:

I can and I will.

Carpe diem.

I've got this.

The Truth about Photos

It's not uncommon for people to compare themselves to images they see in magazines, movies, or on the Internet. It often looks like the people in those pictures have perfect faces and bodies, but here's an important thing you should know—what you see in pictures and on the screen is not always realistic. In reality, the faces and bodies of those people have normal features and shapes—just like yours. Many images in these **mediums** have been altered or airbrushed to minimize the appearance of so-called "imperfections."

But altering photos is nothing new! The photo to the right shows General Ulysses S. Grant on a horse in front of troops during the Civil War. The image was created when Levin Corbin Handy took negatives of three different images to make the one you see here.

Addictions and Chemical Substances

Everyone has the potential to become addicted—be it to social media, video games, junk food, or even more dangerous things, such as alcohol or drugs.

Addiction happens in the brain. When you experience something that your brain perceives as pleasurable, it emits a chemical called **dopamine**. This in turn makes your body crave more of that particular substance or activity. But the next time, your brain secretes less dopamine, so you need more of that substance or activity. In fact, each time you give in to that craving, you need larger and larger amounts of it to feel the same level of satisfaction. And continually giving in to those cravings forms a habit.

But just because you enjoy doing something doesn't necessarily mean it is an addiction. So how can you tell if you or others around you have addictions? If someone's behavior interferes with their health or their relationships, then it might be an addiction. Consider these questions to determine whether a particular behavior is an addiction.

- Does the behavior interfere with your sleep?
- Does the behavior interfere with getting your homework done?
- Can you quit the behavior "cold turkey" (stopping suddenly and completely)?
- Does the behavior prevent you from spending time with family and friends?
- Have people commented that you have a problem related to the behavior?

Breaking an Addiction

If you need help breaking an addiction, talk to a school counselor, a doctor, or your parents. Place yourself in environments where you will be held accountable for your behavior and won't feel tempted.

There are some addictions that are more serious than others, such as alcohol or drugs. Addiction to either of these can have severe effects on our bodies. Drinking alcohol slows the reactions in the brain. That impairs judgment and coordination. Long-term abuse of alcohol can lead to many health problems, including heart and central nervous system damage. Marijuana use can temporarily cause drowsiness. It can also create difficulty with problem solving. Chronic marijuana use can affect short-term memory, meaning a person might struggle more to remember daily things.

There are some people who are **genetically predisposed** to certain addictions, such as alcoholism. And the younger a person is when he or she tries a substance, the more likely he or she will develop an addiction to it.

Make a Decision

If you know there will be drugs or alcohol around, make a decision about how to respond ahead of time. By doing this, you are more likely to make safer decisions because you have mentally prepared yourself.

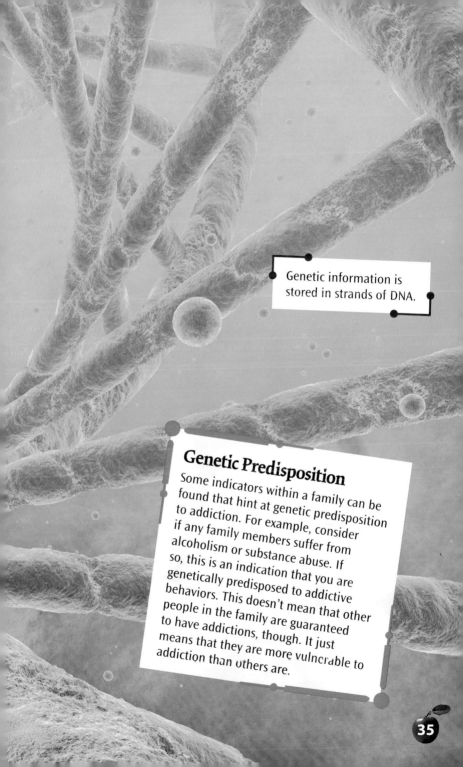

Genetic information is stored in strands of DNA.

Genetic Predisposition

Some indicators within a family can be found that hint at genetic predisposition to addiction. For example, consider if any family members suffer from alcoholism or substance abuse. If so, this is an indication that you are genetically predisposed to addictive behaviors. This doesn't mean that other people in the family are guaranteed to have addictions, though. It just means that they are more vulnerable to addiction than others are.

Healthy Relationships

With so many people in your life, you cannot help but be affected by them and the relationships you have with them. Most likely, there are some people you wish you didn't have relationships with (perhaps an annoying lab partner), and there are others you wish you did have relationships with (a student on the other side of the room). It's no wonder that relationships are among the most important elements of our emotional lives. And because of this, relationships have a lot to do with your happiness and your health.

What's Smell Got to Do with It?

Scientists have spent a lot of time and money studying our noses. Believe it or not, your nose is a primary reason you are attracted to certain people— yes, your nose! Everyone emits chemical substances known as *pheromones*. These are unique to each person, but we don't notice them in the way that we notice sprays or perfumes. Instead, the chemicals affect us unconsciously and influence whether we are attracted to another person. When pheromones float through the air, they stimulate nerves in the nose and then travel to the brain. Then, the brain sends a message to let you know if you are attracted to that person or not—subconsciously of course!

Uncontrollable Attraction

Is being attracted to someone really uncontrollable? Yes, initial attraction is out of your control, but that doesn't mean you will fall in love with everyone you are subconsciously attracted to. In fact, you may be attracted to a person whom you will never meet, so a meaningful relationship might never develop. Regardless of what our brain chemicals may be trying to tell us, we always have a choice about what we do.

It's important to be connected to other people. Family, friends, and significant others hold important roles in our lives. The chemicals in your body, such as dopamine, **serotonin**, and **oxytocin**, provide those feelings of being connected, in love, and loved by others. These feelings do not have to be romantic; they also include the connections to and love you feel toward your family and friends.

If you find yourself unhappy in a relationship for an extended length of time, then it's probably not a healthy relationship. Sometimes this is due to lack of good communication—people not being honest about what they want from the relationship. You may find that the relationship is not a healthy one because there are unreasonable demands placed on you. These are all clues that it's probably best to move on and seek healthier, happier relationships. Or it can be due to the "feel-good" chemicals wearing off over time. These chemicals will let you know if a relationship is a good one or not. So pay close attention to how you feel.

Breaking Up Is Hard to Do

For a majority of people, there really is no way to end a relationship without hurting the other person. However, it's always best to be honest and as kind as possible. The best rule is to put yourself in the other person's shoes and treat him or her the way you would want to be treated.

Ten Tips for Being Mentally and Physically Healthy!

Remember, you have control over many aspects of your health, wellness, and happiness. Here are some tips.

1 Get some exercise every day.
Exercising daily will help you relieve stress as well as build muscle and improve strength.

2 Learn something new.
Learning new skills or hobbies helps you become a more creative and well-rounded person.

3 Always do your best.
Even if you fail at some things, you will have the satisfaction of trying and doing the best that you can in any situation.

4 Be the encouraging voice in the room.
Everyone loves to be around uplifting people, so be the person everyone likes by sharing encouraging, authentic words.

5 Surround yourself with creative people.
You will become more creative because these people will teach you how to think more creatively.

6 Eat a balanced, nutritious diet.
This will benefit your thinking abilities and your overall health.

7

Find positive people to hang out with.

The people you hang around help shape who you are, so decide to make positive people your friends.

8

Speak positively to yourself.

Being kind to yourself is one of the best ways to boost confidence and help manage stress.

9

When in a tough situation, stick to your values.

This shows what kind of person you are on the inside, and others will feel that they can trust you.

10

Have a sense of humor.

Laughter is a stress reliever and triggers the release of feel-good chemicals, so find things to laugh about every day.

Put in the Time

The best thing you can do is take care of your body and your mind. Taking time to invest in and care for yourself will help you live a happy, positive life. This means learning to identify stress and knowing what to do to keep it from affecting your mind and body. It also includes paying attention to your diet and making sure you get enough nutrient-rich foods. Making time for fitness—be it running, swimming, or playing a sport—is also important for keeping your body at its healthiest.

When confronted with various types of chemical substances, knowing that you are informed and can choose to make the right decisions helps you determine what falls in line with your values and what doesn't. Cultivating relationships that are uplifting and loving will bring positivity and happiness to your life. Consider these important things and treat yourself well—you deserve the very best.

Confidence Is Key

Have you ever heard the saying "Fake it until you make it"? That means to act confident, even though you might not feel it. Over time, acting in this way will naturally result in more confidence.

Glossary

adrenaline—a hormone that makes blood pressure and heart rate increase during an emergency

calories—the amount of energy stored in food

complex carbohydrates—energy sources that break down over time; found in foods such as whole grains, starchy vegetables, potatoes, and brown rice

cortisol—a hormone from the adrenal glands that releases sugar into the bloodstream

dopamine—a chemical that makes the body crave more of a certain feel-good substance or activity

dynamic stretches—stretches that use movement to help extend range of motion

electrolytes—ions in the body that help the flow of nutrients into cells

endorphins—chemicals that the body releases as a reward

genetically predisposed—regarding addiction, those whose brains are wired to respond much quicker to addictive substances

glucose—a sugar in the body that produces energy

hormone—a substance in the body that influences growth or development

legumes—vegetables that grow in pods; examples include beans, lentils, peas, and edamame

macronutrients—the three main sources of calories from food: protein, carbohydrates, and fat

mediums—types of communication

meniscus—cartilage found in the knee that provides stability to the joint

metabolism—the chemical processes by which the body uses food to grow, heal, and make energy

oxytocin—a chemical that provides good feelings, usually relating to love

prefrontal cortex—the section of the brain that makes rational decisions

prolactin—a hormone released when you cry emotional tears

refined—free of impurities

rotator cuffs—the tendons and ligaments found in the shoulder that keep the shoulder joints in place and allow for various movements

serotonin—a chemical that affects mood and social behavior

simple carbohydrates—energy sources that break down quickly; found in foods such as white bread, cakes, fruit, and ice cream

static stretches—stretches that are done while the body is at rest to help lengthen muscles

vigorous—intense or full of energy

Index

Check It Out!

Books

Covey, Sean. 2014. *The 7 Habits of Highly Effective Teens*. Touchstone.

Lingampalli, Krishna. 2013. *Teenager's Guide to Heath and Fitness*. Xlibris.

Murphy, Julie. 2015. *Dumplin'*. Balzer + Bray.

Mysko, Claire. 2008. *Girls Inc. Presents You're Amazing!: A No-Pressure Guide to Being Your Best Self*. Adams Media.

Thomas, Bonnie. 2011. *Creative Expression Activities for Teens: Exploring Identity through Art, Craft, and Journaling*. Jessica Kingsley Publishers.

Vizzini, Ned. 2007. *It's Kind of a Funny Story*. Miramax Books.

Video

PBS/Sarah Spinks. *Frontline: Inside the Teenage Brain*.

Websites

Teen Ink. http://www.teenink.com/.

Young Composers. http://www.youngcomposers.com/.

Try It!

Create a poster of various affirmations that you want to remind yourself of on a daily basis. Use the following steps to help you.

- Think of some healthy choices you currently make. They can involve your identity, physical health, mental health, or relationships.

- What are some healthy choices you would like to start making?

- Look at both lists and think of positive quotations that you could say daily to inspire yourself to keep making healthy choices and/or start making new healthy choices.

- If you cannot think of any, research some famous or historical people that you admire. Can you find a positive affirmation from a book, a speech, or a song about your chosen person?

- Once you have at least five quotations, use them to make a poster. Make sure the words are bold and visible. You can write each letter by hand or cut letters out of newspapers or magazines.

- When your affirmations are on your board, decorate the rest of the board with healthy, inspirational images or drawings.

- Hang your poster somewhere easily visible so that you can see it daily.

About the Author

Wendy Conklin has spent the last 15 years honing her skills as a writer for both teachers and students. She is always looking for ways to be creative in both her writing and in the things she chooses to do in her everyday life. She lives with the belief that the secret to being creative is to put oneself in situations of learning new skills. She spends much of her time learning new skills such as upholstering, drawing, and playing the guitar. Her next endeavor will most likely be photography.